6. Pray for God's help. You *need* God's help in order to understand what you study in the Bible. Psalm 119:18 would be an appropriate verse for you to take to God in prayer.

7. *Class teachers using this course for group study will find some helpful suggestions on page 47.*

how to take the self-check tests

Each lesson is concluded with a test designed to help you evaluate what you have learned.

1. Review the lesson carefully in the light of the self-check test questions.

2. If there are any questions in the self-check test you cannot answer, perhaps you have written into your lesson the wrong answer from your Bible. Go over your work carefully to make sure you have filled in the blanks correctly.

3. When you think you are ready to take the self-check test, do so without looking up the answers.

4. Check your answers to the self-check test carefully with the answer key given on page 48.

5. If you have any questions wrong, your answer key will tell you where to find the correct answer in your lesson. Go back and locate the right answers. Learn by your mistakes!

apply what you have learned to your own life

In this connection, read carefully JAMES 1:22-25. It is only as you apply your lessons to your own life that you will really grow in grace and increase in the knowledge of God.

The Christian

"Without me ye can _Nothing_____."

In considering subjects having to do with Christian ethics and practical Christian service, it is first necessary to understand that the teachings of the Lord Jesus Christ are not to be separated from Christ Himself.

The beginning of the Christian life

1. Why is it impossible for the unsaved man to live the Christian life?

I CORINTHIANS 2:14 _Can't understand what God_

2. Why can't man live the Christian life by obeying the Ten Commandments?

ROMANS 8:3, 4 _____

3. What is the first essential for Christian living?

COLOSSIANS 1:27 _Christ in You._

4. A Christian, then, is not simply one who is endeavoring to live a moral life and do good works, but one who is trusting in the Lord Jesus for salvation by _God's Grace_.

EPHESIANS 2:8, 9

Assurance of salvation

The faithfulness of God assures salvation.

5. It is the Father's will that _we believe in Christ to have eternal life_. JOHN 6:39, 40

6. The Christian is eternally secure in Christ because he is

sealed with _The (Holy Spirit Promis_
EPHESIANS 1:13

7. He _hears_ his Shepherd's voice and _follow_
Him and is therefore secured unto the end by the grasp of the

hand of _the fathe_ and of the _son_ . JOHN 10:27-29

8. He is _God's Power for th salvation_ .
I PETER 1:5

9. Upon whom must one constantly depend for enabling
power?

a. ACTS 1:8 _Holy Spirit for Christ_

b. PHILIPPIANS 1:6 _Christ_

10. Although the believer will have his old, sinful nature
until he goes to be with Christ, how should he regard it in
this life?

GALATIANS 2:20 _____

The believer and good works

11. What is the true basis of good works?

EPHESIANS 2:8, 10 _____

12. The believer's good works are the *proof* of what?

JAMES 2:17, 18_____

13. One who has been born of the Holy Spirit will be "careful"
to do what?

TITUS 3:5-8 _____

14. Who alone can make the believer capable of every good work?

Hebrews 13:20, 21_____

15. What can a redeemed soul always say?

Philippians 4:13_____

_____

Growth in the Christian life

16. The power of the old nature can be broken in the life

only by_____.

Galatians 5:16

17. What is the fruit of the Spirit? It can be produced only by His indwelling power.

Galatians 5:22, 23_____

_____

18. To manifest the life that is "created in righteousness and

true holiness," the Christian must be_____

_____. Ephesians 4:23

19. What is God's will for every Christian?

Colossians 3:1, 2_____

20. How is obedience to this command experienced?

Romans 12:2_____

21. What is one Biblical command about Christian growth?

II Peter 3:18 _____

_____

22. What is essential to spiritual growth?

I Peter 2:2 _____

Note: It is not merely reading the Bible that brings spiritual development. It is owning the authority of the Word of God and being obedient to what it says that counts.

23. Since sin hinders growth, it should be removed. What is one essential to a cleansed life?

Psalm 119:9 _____

24. Fruit-bearing by the Christian depends upon what relationship?

John 15:4 _____

25. With such prospects as these, what is the only logical response from the Christian?

a. Romans 12:1 _____

_____

b. I Corinthians 15:58 _____

_____

check-up time No. 1

You have just studied some important truths about the Christian life. Review your study by rereading the questions and your written answers. If you aren't sure of an answer, reread the Scripture portion given to see if you can find the answer. Then take the following test to see how well you understand important truths you have studied.

In the right-hand margin write "True" or "False" after each of the following statements.

1. A Christian is simply one who is endeavoring to live a moral life. _____

2. Good works should be the outgrowth of faith. _____

3. An unsaved man can live a Christian life. _____

4. The Christian is kept saved by his own strength. _____

5. The Holy Spirit has sealed the believer; therefore, his salvation is secure. _____

6. Christ has provided sufficient strength for us to live victoriously for Him. _____

7. A person's way can be cleansed if he takes heed to the Word of God. _____

8. Fruit-bearing depends upon abiding in Christ. _____

9. Victory over the old, sinful nature comes by walking in the Spirit. _____

10. A Christian should present his body a living sacrifice to God. _____

Turn to page 48 and check your answers.

Humility

"Before honor is_____."

PROVERBS 15:33

Christ, the perfect Example of humility

1. What could the Son of God say of Himself?

MATTHEW 11:29 _____

Only the Lord Jesus could make such a statement concerning Himself.

2. What does Paul tell us concerning the self-humbling of the Son of God?

He "made himself _____

_____

_____

_____

_____." PHILIPPIANS 2:6-8

3. What lowly service did the Son of God render following the last Passover supper?

JOHN 13:1-5 _____

4. What argument preceded this act?

LUKE 22:24 _____

5. Who was among those whose feet Jesus washed?

JOHN 13:11 _____

God's approval of the contrite, humble spirit

6. "Though the LORD be high, yet _____

_____." PSALM 138:6

7. Unto whom does "the high and lofty One" draw near?

ISAIAH 57:15 _____

Humility and the Christian life

8. What bearing does this Christian characteristic have on effectual prayer?

PSALM 10:17; compare ISAIAH 66:2_____

_____

9. Whose prayer will God not forget?

PSALM 9:12 _____

10. Who has least difficulty in discerning the will of God?

PSALM 25:9 _____

11. Who has the best chance of becoming spiritually beautiful?

PSALM 149:4 _____

12. Who is likely to lay hold of true wisdom?

PROVERBS 11:2_____

13. What is the path to true riches, honor and life?

PROVERBS 22:4; compare 29:23_____

_____

14. Who has the promise of God's grace?

PROVERBS 3:34; compare JAMES 4:6_____

15. Who has the promise of an increase of joy in the LORD?

ISAIAH 29:19_____

16. Why do some never understand spiritual things?

LUKE 10:21 _____

17. How can true greatness be won?

MATTHEW 20:26, 27_____

Humility and Christian love

Humility does not consist in thinking humbly of one's self so much as in not thinking of self at all—and in thinking of Christ more and more.

18. When one really begins to know Christ, what will he desire above all else?

PHILIPPIANS 2:5 _____

19. How does a humble Christian regard others?

a. ROMANS 12:3 _____

_____

b. ROMANS 12:10_____

_____

20. How does the love of Christ affect a person?

I CORINTHIANS 13:4_____

21. What is God's way to greatness?

MATTHEW 23:11, 12_____

22. What does a humble Christian refuse to do?

PROVERBS 27:2_____

23. What does he not desire?

GALATIANS 5:26 _____

24. What is the glory of the humble soul?

GALATIANS 6:14 _____

25. How does this spirit work in the Church?

EPHESIANS 5:21; PHILIPPIANS 2:3, 4_____

_____

26. How does it manifest itself in Christian leaders?

I PETER 5:3_____

27. What does the humble Christian avoid?

JEREMIAH 45:5 _____

28. What is certain to create a sense of the Christian's insufficiency?
ISAIAH 51:1 _____

_____

29. When one of humble spirit has attained recognized success in service, how does he still feel?

LUKE 17:10 _____

30. What, therefore, should be the desire of the believer?

a. COLOSSIANS 3:12_____

b. I PETER 5:6_____

You have just studied some important truths about humility. Review your study by rereading the questions and your written answers. If you aren't sure of an answer, reread the Scripture portion given to see if you can find the answer. Then take the following test to see how well you understand important truths you have studied.

In the right-hand margin write "True" or "False" after each of the following statements.

1. A humble Christian recognizes that, at best, he is an unprofitable servant. _____

2. Humility is necessary for effectual prayer. _____

3. One becomes great by being a servant of others. _____

4. The genuine humility of the disciples showed through when they washed the feet of Jesus. _____

5. A humble Christian praises himself. _____

6. A humble Christian disregards the feelings of others. _____

7. God tends to overlook the prayers of humble people. _____

8. A humble Christian will always be seeking great things for himself. _____

9. God draws near to the humble. _____

10. The humble soul glories in the cross of Christ. _____

Turn to page 48 and check your answers.

Love

"The greatest of these is_____."

I Corinthians 13:13

The "love chapters" of the New Testament

There are two "love chapters" in the New Testament—
I John 4 and I Corinthians 13.

I John 4

1. Why is love expected of a Christian?

Verse 7_____

_____

2. What might well be evidenced by a lack of the spirit of love?

Verse 8_____

3. By showing_____we give evi-

dence that God dwells in us and we in_____. Verses 12, 13

4. What will divine love in the heart abolish?

Verse 18 _____

5. Who is said to be a liar?

Verse 20 _____

6. He who truly loves God _____

_____. VERSE 21

I CORINTHIANS 13

In this chapter we have a spiritual clinic on love. Note that the Greek word translated by the old English word "charity" in our Authorized Version should be "love." It is a purely Christian word: no example of its use occurs in the Greek classics by any heathen writer. The word denotes a love which has nothing of the sensual in it. It is a purely spiritual love, in contrast to all human conceptions of love.

7. What is better than all the Christian gifts?

VERSE 1; compare I CORINTHIANS 12:31 _____

8. What is God's estimate of one who does not manifest love, though he may be greatly gifted in other ways?

VERSE 2 _____

9. Can a lavish hand take the place of a loving heart?

VERSE 3 _____

10. Is it possible that even martyrdom can be ventured with other motives than love?

VERSE 3 _____

11. How will divine love show through in the life of a true Christian?

VERSE 4 _____

_____

12. What effect does this love have on outward manners?

VERSE 5 _____

13. What are four things foreign to true love?
VERSE 5

a. _____

b. _____

c. _____

d. _____

The word rendered "easily provoked" ("easily" is not expressed in the original at all) means, literally, "not exasperated." On no occasion does love "fly off the handle."

14. Can real love ever allow one to be glad when someone else goes wrong?

VERSE 6 _____

15. In what does love always rejoice?

VERSE 6 _____

16. In what four ways is love manifested according to verse 7?

a. _____

b. _____

c. _____

d. _____

The meaning of the word rendered "beareth" is that one does not flame with resentment against an injurer.

17. What never fails?

VERSE 8 _____

18. The highest affection of the soul is_____. VERSE 13

Love in action

19. Love will cause one to be_____

_____. ROMANS 12:10

20. Where love divine reigns we will_____

_____. COLOSSIANS 3:13

21. Love for the brethren is an evidence of what?

I JOHN 3:14 _____

22. What of those who give no thought to people about them who are in need?

I JOHN 3:17 _____

23. Will true love be merely emotional?

I JOHN 3:18 _____

24. What can the love implanted by the Holy Spirit enable a Christian to do?

LUKE 6:35_____

25. What is one way whereby the world will know that we are true followers of Christ?

JOHN 13:35 _____

26. If we have Christ's love, we will be_____

_____. EPHESIANS 4:32

27. "If God so loved us,_____

_____." I JOHN 4:11

check-up time No. 3

You have just studied some important truths about the nature of love in the Christian life. Review your study by rereading the questions and your written answers. If you aren't sure of an answer, reread the Scripture portion given to see if you can find the answer. Then take the following test to see how well you understand important truths you have studied.

In the right-hand margin write "True" or "False" after each of the following statements.

1. Love is easily provoked.   _____

2. Being benevolent can take the place of love.   _____

3. One who truly loves God loves his brother.   _____

4. If we have Christ's love, we will forgive others. _____

5. The complete lack of the spirit of love is an evidence that one does not know God.   _____

6. Outward manners are affected by love.   _____

7. In God's sight one who does not manifest love is nothing.   _____

8. Real love allows one to be glad when someone else goes wrong.   _____

9. Love implanted by the Holy Spirit enables us to love our enemies.   _____

10. Love is the greatest Christian quality.   _____

Turn to page 48 and check your answers.

Purity

"Blessed are the _____

_____." MATTHEW 5:8

Purity—a requirement of God

1. "Thou shalt not_____."
EXODUS 20:14

2. To what is every Christian called?

I PETER 1:15_____
The word rendered "conversation" means "manner of life."

3. As children of God, we should not_____

_____. I PETER 1:14

4. What should every Christian keep constantly in mind?

I THESSALONIANS 4:7 _____

5. What injunction did Paul give to Christians regarding persons known to be fornicators?

I CORINTHIANS 5:11; compare PROVERBS 2:20_____

_____

The source of temptation

6. What is one source of evil desires?

MARK 7:21 _____

7. What are some of the works of the flesh?

GALATIANS 5:19-21 _____

_____

"Lasciviousness" means "sexual vice."

8. What do fleshly lusts do?

I PETER 2:11_____

9. What draws a person into sin?

JAMES 1:13-15 _____

_____

The subtlety of lustful temptation

10. How do lustful women often practice their wiles?

a. PROVERBS 5:3 _____

b. PROVERBS 6:25 _____

c. PROVERBS 7:21 _____

11. What does the fornicator do?

I CORINTHIANS 6:18_____

12. To what is the man likened who yields to such lustful wiles?

PROVERBS 7:22_____

It goes without saying that the same is true of a woman who listens to the pleadings of an evil-minded man.

13. Are impurity and immorality worse than covetousness?

EPHESIANS 5:3-8 _____

14. Can one be guilty of sins of impurity in God's sight even before actual indulgence?

MATTHEW 5:28_____

18

15. "The world passeth away and_____

_____." I JOHN 2:17

It is important to remember that sins of the disposition are just as serious as sins of actual misconduct. (Read the story of the prodigal son, Luke 15:11-32, and note that the *attitude* of the elder brother estranged him from the father just as much as the *actions* of the younger.)

God's provision in temptation

16. How does one who is planning impurity usually deceive himself?

JOB 24:15 _____

17. Although deceiving himself, why does he not deceive God?

PROVERBS 5:21_____

_____

18. What provision has been made for meeting temptation?

I CORINTHIANS 10:13 _____

19. In a time of temptation, to whom should we turn for help?

ROMANS 7:24, 25_____

The Christian's responsibility

20. Why is it important for the Christian to guard the use of his body?

I CORINTHIANS 3:16; 6:19 _____

_____

21. What is the Christian to do?

a. ROMANS 13:14 _____

b. PHILIPPIANS 4:8 _____

---

22. With what should the tempted one fill his mind?

PSALM 119:9, 11 _____

God cannot use us if we are indifferent to the claims of purity. Only the pure in heart can have spiritual discernment. One is in a sad decline whose soul shows no concern to keep itself unspotted. (See I Corinthians 6:19, 20.)

One can no more filter the mind into purity than he can compress it into calmness. To have it pure, it must be given over to the control of the Holy Spirit, and the things of impurity avoided. Guard it if you would have your heart pure. Store it full of the pure truth of God's Word.

check-up time No. 4

You have just studied some important truths about God's requirement of chastity. Review your study by rereading the questions and your written answers. If you aren't sure of an answer, reread the Scripture portion given to see if you can find the answer. Then take the following test to see how well you understand important truths you have studied.

In the right-hand margin write "True" or "False" after each of the following statements.

1. Temptation never arises from within the heart. _____

2. The heart is one source of temptation. _____

3. A Christian is called to live a holy life. _____

4. Some acts can be hidden from God. _____

5. Submitting to God's Word will help us be victorious in times of temptation. _____

6. Fleshly lusts war against the soul. _____

7. In times of temptation, we should immediately turn to Christ for help. _____

8. The Christian's body is the temple of the Holy Spirit. _____

9. Christians should keep company with immoral people. _____

10. Mental acts of impurity are all right, but outward acts of impurity are wrong. _____

Turn to page 48 and check your answers.

Integrity

Do "as ye would that_____

_____." LUKE 6:31

The Bible demands integrity

1. God requires that we_____

_____. ZECHARIAH 8:16

2. A basic principle of Christianity demands that we provide

_____. ROMANS 12:17

3. Provide for "_____, not only in

the sight of the Lord, but_____

_____." II CORINTHIANS 8:21

One of the first things expected of a Christian is absolute integrity, conformity to the basic laws of God concerning honesty and uprightness.

4. Two things that are an abomination to the Lord are_____

_____. PROVERBS 20:10

5. Ye shall not_____

_____. LEVITICUS 19:11

These divine requirements are not flexible. They cover such sins as overcharging, under-paying, short-weighting, skimping of work for which one is paid.

6. What does a righteous man despise?

PROVERBS 13:5_____

God hates "a lying tongue"

7. "Seven . . . things doth the LORD hate." PROVERBS 6:16-19

a. _____

b. _____

c. _____

d. _____

e. _____

f. _____

g. _____

8. Lying usually manifests itself_____

_____. PSALM 58:3

9. With false dealing go_____

_____. LEVITICUS 19:11

10. What two things are forbidden?   PROVERBS 24:28

a. _____

b. _____

11. Those who love lies belong with_____

_____. REVELATION 22:15

12. The father of lies is_____. JOHN 8:44

13. One of the basic laws of God is that_____

_____. Leviticus 25:14

14. "Let him that_____:

but rather let him_____

_____

_____." Ephesians 4:28

15. What is said of the lying tongue?

Proverbs 12:19 _____

_____

Lies are bound to collapse in time. They are difficult to maintain, for more lies are told to cover up the first one. Make a lie your refuge, and you will have no permanent shelter.

The Christian represents his Lord

16. If you are a Christian, you are the world's Bible, an epistle

_____. II Corinthians 3:2

17. The way to silence those who criticize Christianity is to

_____. I Peter 2:12
"Conversation" here means "manner of living."

18. A true child of God will use_____

_____. Leviticus 19:36

24

19. What are some essentials of being strictly honest?

DEUTERONOMY 25:13-16_____

_____

_____

20. If you cannot do well financially without resorting to deceit, nevertheless, as a poor man, you are_____

_____. PROVERBS 19:22

God will judge

21. "There is nothing covered, that_____

_____; neither hid,_____

_____." LUKE 12:2

22. Woe unto him that_____

_____. JEREMIAH 22:13

23. What does God say of a false witness?

PROVERBS 19:5_____

_____

24. The LORD delights in those who_____

_____. PROVERBS 12:22

25. Some people boast of their ability to tell lies (PSALM 52:1-5).

Of such, God says:_____

_____

_____. VERSE 5

26. Heaven is not to be the home of_____

_____. REVELATION 21:27

"Put away lying"

27. What is one prayer a Christian should earnestly pray?

PSALM 119:29, 30_____

28. Why should Christians have nothing to do with lies?

COLOSSIANS 3:9, 10_____

_____

29. Put away lying and_____

_____. EPHESIANS 4:25

30. What hinders the prayers of many people?

ISAIAH 59:1-3 _____

_____

31. Is a Christian expected to overcome evil habits in his own strength?

JUDE 24_____

Love righteousness for Christ's sake

Two basic propositions for every Christian:

a. Be sure that all you possess is obtained honestly.

b. Be sure to speak only truth.

It seems a simple thing to tell the truth; but, beyond question, there is nothing half so easy as lying. It is one of the first sins manifested in a child.

Cultivate the loftiest integrity even in the smallest matters, remembering that the world judges Christ by what you do as a professing Christian. Prove to all that you deal squarely, not merely for the sake of your reputation, but because of a sense of obligation to your Lord and because He causes you to love righteousness.

check-up time No. 5

You have just studied some important truths about the need for integrity and dependability in 'the Christian life. Review your study by rereading the questions and your written answers. If you aren't sure of an answer, reread the Scripture portion given to see if you can find the answer. Then take the following test to see how well you understand important truths you have studied.

In the right-hand margin write "True" or "False" after each of the following statements.

1. Living a godly life can help to silence those who criticize Christianity. _____

2. A Christian should ask God to keep him from the way of lying. _____

3. It is better to be rich at any cost than to be poor. _____

4. Many people know what the Bible says only as they watch the life of a Christian. _____

5. Christians should practice deception if "the end justifies the means." _____

6. Lying manifests itself in a very young child. _____

7. The devil is the father of lies. _____

8. In Revelation 22:15 lying is classed with murder. _____

9. Prayer can be successful even though there is unconfessed and deliberately cherished sin in the life. _____

10. God will some day make known and judge all unconfessed and hence unforgiven sin. _____

Turn to page 48 and check your answers.

Generosity

"It is more blessed to give_____

_____." Acts 20:35

The Biblical principle

1. What is a divine principle of giving?

Proverbs 3:9, 10 _____

_____

2. Since we have received freely from God, what should we do?

Matthew 10:8_____

3. What is one test of whether or not the love of God dwells in a person?

I John 3:17 _____

_____

_____

4. What proportion of the Israelites' income did God require for His house?

Malachi 3:10 _____

5. What did God promise to do for those who *began* by giving ten per cent of their income?

Malachi 3:10 _____

_____

6. Is God able to keep those who honor Him with their increase from being in want?

MALACHI 3:11 _____

Some professing Christians' response to God's will about giving might be stated like this: "Pour out Thy blessings; and after we have satisfied all our wants, real and fancied, and have provided for the future, we will contribute an occasional dime—if we happen to be present when the offering is taken." It must be remembered constantly that God wants more than our money. Note that the Macedonian Christians were commended because they "first gave their own selves to the Lord." (Read II Corinthians 8:1-5.) Giving money to God is of no value unless we first give ourselves unreservedly to Him.

7. Who gives us the power to acquire wealth?

DEUTERONOMY 8:17, 18 _____

A bountiful return

8. What is one vital Christian principle?

II CORINTHIANS 9:6 _____

_____

9. What is our Lord's promise?

LUKE 6:38 _____

_____

_____

10. What does God never forget?

HEBREWS 6:10 _____

_____

11. What kind of reward will be reserved for those who are really sacrificial givers?

LUKE 6:35_____

12. What is one condition of having the full blessing of God upon our lives?

ISAIAH 58:10, 11 _____

_____

13. What is one condition of having "the glory of the LORD" in one's life?

ISAIAH 58:7, 8 _____

_____

14. What is one way of discovering real happiness?

PROVERBS 14:21 _____

15. What is one doing when he has pity on the needy?

PROVERBS 19:17 _____
According to this verse, how will such an investment be

repaid? _____

_____

16. What is one way of overcoming enemies?

PROVERBS 25:21 _____

_____

17. In time of trouble, what does God promise to do for him who considers the poor?

PSALM 41:1 _____

18. What is one way to merit true honor before men?

PSALM 112:9_____

19. How is all such Christian ministry registered in heaven?

MATTHEW 25:40 _____

20. What definite assurance is given us?

GALATIANS 6:9_____

21. What is promised to the person who is a liberal giver?

PROVERBS 11:25 _____

22. What is promised to the person who gives without display? ("Openly" is not found in the best Greek texts.)

MATTHEW 6:4 _____

How much shall we give?

23. What is the test of how much the Christian should give?

DEUTERONOMY 16:17 _____

_____

24. What is the gauge of his responsibility?

LUKE 12:48 _____

_____

25. If the believer does not give at least a tithe, of what may he be guilty?

MALACHI 3:8_____

26. What may the believer often give over and above the tithe, as God has prospered him?

MALACHI 3:8, last phrase _____

God's claim on our time and income is for our good. He makes the tithe the minimum of what is reasonable, not because *He* is in need, but because *we* need to give.

27. What rule did Paul suggest for New Testament believers?

I CORINTHIANS 16:2_____ _____

28. If we give "as God hath prospered" us, is it likely that He expects less of us than of an Israelite under the dispensation of law?

II CORINTHIANS 8:1-3_____

God is concerned, not so much about the amount we *give*, as about what we have left (MARK 12:41-44).

29. Can one afford, for his own sake, to give on a lower scale than that required of a Jew in Old Testament times?

PROVERBS 3:9, 10_____

30. Are people likely to be dependent on the public dole because of having given "tithes and offerings" for God's work?

PROVERBS 11:24 _____

What is the true spirit?

31. What should be the basic motive for all giving?

I CORINTHIANS 13:3_____

32. What negative attitude should we avoid?

DEUTERONOMY 15:10 _____

33. What twofold attitude does not please God?

II CORINTHIANS 9:7

a. _____

b. _____

34. What kind of giver does God especially love?

II CORINTHIANS 9:7_____

check-up time No. 6

You have just studied some important truths about the grace of giving. Review your study by rereading the questions and your written answers. If you aren't sure of an answer, reread the Scripture portion given to see if you can find the answer. Then take the following test to see how well you understand important truths you have studied.

In the right-hand margin write "True" or "False" after each of the following statements.

1. Generosity should be shown only to our friends. _____

2. Man has the power within himself to acquire wealth. _____

3. The expected reward is the only motive for giving. _____

4. Our giving should be done cheerfully. _____

5. The Christian's generosity to others is looked upon by God as generosity to Christ. _____

6. Giving of necessity is a good motive for showing generosity. _____

7. God has promised abundant blessing to those who give a tithe of their income to His work. _____

8. God always gives in return far more than we give to Him. _____

9. We are asked to give in proportion to the way God has prospered us. _____

10. God required at least one-tenth of the income of Israel. _____

Turn to page 48 and check your answers.

Steadfastness

"Be ye_____

_____." I Corinthians 15:58

Suffering for Christ's sake

1. When we are faced with trial, we are not to think_____

_____

_____. I Peter 4:12

2. Tribulation worketh_____. Romans 5:3
The word "patience" means "endurance," "fortitude," or "steadfastness."

3. The Christian should never be given the impression that

he is appointed unto a life of comfort and ease, for_____

_____

_____. Philippians 1:29

4. The believer who discerns anything of what Christ has suffered on his behalf will desire, not only to know Him and

the power of His resurrection, but also to know_____

_____. Philippians 3:10

5. Those who expect to reign with Christ may also expect to

_____. II Timothy 2:12

34

6. If we are to be joint heirs with Jesus Christ, we should be

willing to _____

_____. ROMANS 8:17

7. He who is unwilling to take up his cross and follow the Lord

Jesus is_____. MATTHEW 10:38

8. If the world has persecuted Christ_____

_____. JOHN 15:20, 21

9. Whether the Christian's "purging" (JOHN 15:2) takes the form of persecution, bodily affliction, or perplexities, of one

thing he can ever be confident, that_____

_____. ROMANS 8:28

10. In Christ we can always_____
                                II CORINTHIANS 2:14

His grace_____. II CORINTHIANS 12:9

Why people suffer

Hereditary suffering is the common lot of a fallen race.

11. What is the universal effect of the sin of Adam?

ROMANS 5:12 _____

12. Do certain types of sin carry penalties which affect future generations?

EXODUS 20:5_____

_____

Judicial suffering comes upon the lost as a direct penalty for evil-doing. It covers two realms—here and hereafter.

13. How does one manufacture cords for his own binding?

PROVERBS 5:22_____

14. What do men often suffer in their own bodies?

ROMANS 1:27_____

Corrective suffering is God's chastening, or child-training, for those in His family, that is, the redeemed.

15. Who can be certain of chastening if he goes against his best light?

HEBREWS 12:5-7 _____

16. What is a good indication that one who lives in sin, unchecked by God, is not His child?

HEBREWS 12:8_____

_____

17. In some instances, what does the Father do with His own children?

I CORINTHIANS 5:5 _____

_____

Why? _____

_____

18. Why are God's children chastened in this life?

I CORINTHIANS 11:32 _____

Preparatory suffering is intended to fit God's people for closer fellowship with Him and more effective service—to produce patience, humility, love and other Christian graces.

19. What can we learn by the things which we suffer?

HEBREWS 5:8 _____

20. What may affliction produce in one who accepts it by faith?

II CORINTHIANS 4:17 _____

21. What should be our attitude in suffering?

I PETER 4:13_____

_____

Suffering or trial in the life of the Christian does not neces-
sarily mean that he has sinned. It may mean that God is
preparing him for more usefulness in the future.

God's love is farsighted. The Great Physician never gives the
wrong remedy. Physical weakness may be necessary to the
soul's health.

Voluntary suffering is that which one assumes as a servant of
Christ, out of loyalty to Him.

22. Of such suffering the apostle Paul wrote: "I . . . fill up

_____

_____." COLOSSIANS 1:23, 24

Such suffering can be avoided by those who do not care to
risk deeper fellowship with Christ.

23. This is voluntary suffering:

a. For the sake of_____. MATTHEW 5:10

b. For the sake of_____. MATTHEW 5:11

24. Such suffering brings present rejoicing in the knowledge

that_____. MATTHEW 5:12

The ministry of suffering

25. Affliction is often the guide to reflection and the parent

of repentance. "It is good for me_____

_____." PSALM 119:67, 71

26. We can always be sure that_____

_____. PSALM 119:75

27. God would have no hot furnaces if there were no gold to be separated from the dross. "He knoweth_____

_____

_____." JOB 23:10

28. Many Christian graces thrive best under trial; therefore, we should

a. "Let _____

_____." JAMES 1:3, 4

b. Always remember that the "afterward"_____

_____. HEBREWS 12:11

29. There is no Gethsemane without its comforting angel. We are "comforted in all our tribulation, that_____

_____

_____." II CORINTHIANS 1:3, 4

30. As our sufferings abound for Jesus' sake, so_____

_____. II CORINTHIANS 1:5

31. Our trials can be the seed of future glories. We may reckon on the fact that_____

_____. ROMANS 8:18

32. If we walk the path of His will here, we shall find_____

_____. PSALM 16:11

33. Therefore, in the endurance of our trials, our thought should be that we might_____

_____. I PETER 1:7

check-up time No. 7

You have just studied some important truths about faithfulness to Christ. Review your study by re-reading the questions and your written answers. If you aren't sure of an answer, reread the Scripture portion given to see if you can find the answer. Then take the following test to see how well you understand important truths you have studied.

In the right-hand margin write "True" or "False" after each of the following statements.

1. We are better able to comfort others when we have remained steadfast through our own troubles.

2. All suffering by the Christian is the result of his sin.

3. Although the world persecuted the Lord Jesus, Christians need not expect that it will persecute them.

4. Trial should be considered as foreign to the Christian life.

5. One purpose of tribulation in the life of the Christian is to develop steadfastness.

6. Those who expect to reign with Christ must also expect to suffer with Him.

7. The grace of God is sufficient for forgiveness of our sins, but not for victory in a time of trial.

8. It should be our desire, not only to know Christ and the power of His resurrection, but also to know the fellowship of His sufferings.

9. The proper way to react to suffering is to complain about it.

10. Our chastisement by God shows that we are His children.

Turn to page 48 and check your answers.

Turn to page 48 and check your answers.

Devotional Life

"True worshippers shall worship the Father

_____."

Much is involved in the worship of God. Many think that all is included in church-going and the saying of prayers. Scripture shows that there are at least four experiences of the devotional life: adoration, thanksgiving, petition and meditation.

Adoration

1. Only_____is to be worshiped. MATTHEW 4:10

2. What did Peter refuse?

ACTS 10:25, 26_____
We may _admire_ men, but we _worship_ only Deity.

3. What did an angel refuse?

REVELATION 22:8, 9_____

4. For whom do angels reserve their worship?

HEBREWS 1:6 _____

5. How many will one day bow the knee to our Lord and Saviour?

PHILIPPIANS 2:9, 10_____

_____

6. How is the Son to be honored?

JOHN 5:23_____

7. How do all heavenly hosts regard our risen Lord?

REVELATION 5:11, 12 _____

_____

_____

8. When one has caught a glimpse of our holy God, how does he feel about himself?

ISAIAH 6:5_____

_____

9. Of what does he always feel the need?

ISAIAH 6:6, 7_____

10. If our hearts are truly fixed on eternal things, what can we say now with all the hosts in heaven?

REVELATION 7:12_____

_____

_____

11. Which of these four experiences of the devotional life is given first place in the prayer our Lord taught His disciples?

MATTHEW 6:9 _____

12. In true adoration, the believer can pray:_____

_____

_____

_____PSALM 139:23, 24

13. The closer one's fellowship with God in the devotional life, the more deeply he is affected by His holiness; therefore, with Paul, he desires that he may_____

_____. PHILIPPIANS 3:10

14. His overwhelming desire is that_____

_____. II CORINTHIANS 4:10, 11

15. One may know that he is in an attitude of worship when he instinctively prays:

a. "Examine _____

_____." PSALM 26:2

b. "Cleanse_____." PSALM 19:12

16. A true worshiper will be willing at all times for God to

_____. JOB 31:6

17. A great part of what is called "public worship" is described in Scripture as_____

_____. II TIMOTHY 3:5

Thanksgiving

18. In true worship, prayer will be permeated with_____

_____. PHILIPPIANS 4:6

The primary meaning of "thankful" is "thoughtful"—being mindful of benefits received. There are more thanksgivings than prayers in the Bible. One reason we have little faith is that we do not pause to count our blessings and give praise.

19. What does the psalmist say of this?

PSALM 92:1, 2 _____

_____

20. What exclamation occurs four times in PSALM 107?

_____

21. In what spirit should one enter the house of God?

PSALM 100:4 _____

22. In all our service, what should we do?

COLOSSIANS 3:17 _____

23. What is God's will for us?

I THESSALONIANS 5:18 _____

24. What grieves the heart of Christ?

LUKE 17:15-18 _____

25. What brings the wrath of God upon men?

ROMANS 1:18-21 _____

_____

26. For what should a believer be able to give thanks?

EPHESIANS 5:20; compare ROMANS 8:28; 5:3-5 _____

_____

Petition

The devotional life is not only something more than church attendance and offering up our desires in prayer; it is an offering up of the old self for crucifixion—a look *in* as well as *up*. Petition will take its proper place only when adoration and the accompanying experiences are recognized as primary.

27. What did Moses have to do with saving Israel from being destroyed?

PSALM 106:23 _____

_____

_____

28. In Ezekiel's day God sought for a man who would "make

up _____ and _____ "

before Him "for _____," that He _____

_____. EZEKIEL 22:30

29. We should petition God on behalf of_____

_____. I TIMOTHY 2:1, 2

30. Paul admonishes us to pray "always _____

_____ in the

Spirit . . . watching thereunto with all perseverance_____

_____." EPHESIANS 6:18

We need to remember that worship is commanded of God. We owe it to Him. Without it, our devotional life is seriously out of balance. Petition is occupied with our needs; thanksgiving, with our blessings; and confession, with our faults. Adoration is concerned only with our triune God.

Meditation

31. The Christian's delight should be "in the law of the LORD;

and in his law" he should "_____

_____." PSALM 1:2

32. God said to Joshua: "This book of the law shall not

depart out of thy mouth; but thou shalt_____

_____." JOSHUA 1:8

33. "As newborn babes," we should "desire the_____

_____" that we "_____

_____." I PETER 2:2

34. God said that a king in Israel should read the book of the

law, that he might learn_____

_____. DEUTERONOMY 17:19

check-up time No. 8

You have just studied some important truths about the habit of having a daily Quiet Time with God. Review your study by rereading the questions and your written answers. If you aren't sure of an answer, reread the Scripture portion given to see if you can find the answer. Then take the following test to see how well you understand important truths you have studied.

In the right-hand margin write "True" or "False" after each of the following statements.

1. We should pray for kings and those in authority. _____

2. Meditation on the Word of God should be a delight. _____

3. The Lord Jesus is adored only on earth. _____

4. Adoration is to be directed only toward God. _____

5. Our prayers should be permeated with thanksgiving. _____

6. It is impossible to give thanks for some of the things that happen to us. _____

7. A true worshiper is willing at all times for God to search his heart. _____

8. An angel allowed John to worship him. _____

9. When one truly "sees" the Lord, he sees how sinful he is himself. _____

10. In the prayer our Lord taught to His disciples, the first place is given to petition. _____

Turn to page 48 and check your answers.

Suggestions for class use

1. The class teacher may wish to tear this page from each workbook as the answer key is on the reverse side.

2. The teacher should study the lesson first, filling in the blanks in the workbook. He should be prepared to give help to the class on some of the harder places in the lesson. He should also take the self-check tests himself, check his answers with the answer key and look up any question answered incorrectly.

3. Class sessions can be supplemented by the teacher's giving a talk or leading a discussion on the subject to be studied. The class could then fill in the workbook together as a group, in teams, or individually. If so desired by the teacher, however, this could be done at home. The self-check tests can be done as homework by the class.

4. The self-check tests can be corrected at the beginning of each class session. A brief discussion of the answers can serve as review for the previous lesson.

5. The teacher should motivate and encourage his students. Some public recognition might well be given to class members who successfully complete this course.

Moody Press, a ministry of the Moody Bible Institute, is designed for education, evangelization and edification. If we may assist you in knowing more about Christ and the Christian life, please write us without obligation to:
Moody Press, c/o MLM, Chicago, Illinois 60610.

answer key
to self-check tests

Be sure to look up any questions you answered incorrectly.

Q gives the number of the test *question*.

A gives the correct *answer*.

R *refers* you back to the number of the question in the lesson itself, where the correct answer is to be found.

Mark with an "x" your wrong answers.

TEST 1			TEST 2			TEST 3			TEST 4		
Q	A	R	Q	A	R	Q	A	R	Q	A	R
1	F	4	1	T	29	1	F	13	1	F	6
2	T	11	2	T	8	2	F	9	2	T	6
3	F	1	3	T	17	3	T	6	3	T	2
4	F	8	4	F	3	4	T	26	4	F	17
5	T	6	5	F	22	5	T	3	5	T	22
6	T	15	6	F	19	6	T	12	6	T	8
7	T	23	7	F	9	7	T	8	7	T	19
8	T	24	8	F	27	8	F	14	8	T	20
9	T	16	9	T	7	9	T	24	9	F	5
10	T	25	10	T	24	10	T	7	10	F	14

TEST 5			TEST 6			TEST 7			TEST 8		
Q	A	R	Q	A	R	Q	A	R	Q	A	R
1	T	17	1	F	16	1	T	29	1	T	29
2	T	27	2	F	7	2	F	23	2	T	31
3	F	20	3	F	31	3	F	8	3	F	7
4	T	16	4	T	34	4	F	1	4	T	1
5	F	28	5	T	19	5	T	2	5	T	18
6	T	8	6	F	33	6	T	5	6	F	26
7	T	12	7	T	5	7	F	10	7	T	15
8	T	11	8	T	9	8	T	4	8	F	3
9	F	30	9	T	23	9	F	21	9	T	8
10	T	21	10	T	4	10	T	16	10	F	11

how well did you do?

0-1 wrong answers—excellent work

2-3 wrong answers—review errors carefully

4 or more wrong answers—restudy the lesson before going on to the next one